FLORENCE
AND TUSCANY

Text by

PIERRE LEPROHON

Crescent Books
New York

Translation:
Evelyn Rossiter

End-papers: a typical Tuscan landscape. Title-page: the Campanile dominates Florence, set amongst the hills.

Designed and produced by
Editions Minerva SA

First English edition published by
Editions Minerva SA

Copyright © 1984 by
Minerva Editions S.A., Genève.

This 1984 edition is published
by Crescent Books.
Distributed by Crown Publishers, Inc.

Printed in Italy

Library of Congress Cataloging
in Publication Data

ISBN: 0-517-43945 X

INTRODUCTION

The rise of European civilization owed much to Florence and the province — some would say state — of Tuscany. The art and culture which they generated brought about a new conception of man and the universe, in a land formed by centuries of struggle, as well as by ambitions which drove the sublimation of life to unknown heights.

At the origin of this remarkable accomplishment were the Etruscans, an ethnic group which had probably come from Asia Minor, and whose civilization developed over seven centuries, leaving vestiges which can still be seen today in the modern province of Tuscany. Then midway through the second millenium the ruling Medici family used its power to make Florence and Tuscany the center of a humanism which was to radiate throughout Europe, spreading its art and its forms to the entire continent.

An aura of glorious things remembered now surrounds the monuments and artistic creations which have withstood the ravages of time. An immense vitality is conveyed by the memory of the stone of Florence — in the Giotto campanile, the tower of the Palazzo Vecchio, the walls of the basilicas and the frescoes of the palaces. The

rivalries and crimes, conflicts and hatreds of the centuries which lay behind these marvelous works, are now effaced, rather than proclaimed by them, as the wonders of art blur the contours of history. As the modern visitor stands in awe before this dazzling array of media and styles — from Romanesque to Renaissance, in architecture, painting, sculpture, mosaic, fresco and terra cotta — he is aware only of their esthetic qualities.

And the setting of these Florentine gems is in itself remarkable: the Tuscan landscape, sky and light help in our understanding of how the painters of the Florentine school managed to create such gentle backgrounds and such tender madonnas. Nowhere else in Italy does the atmosphere have the purity, or the sky the luminous quality to be found in central Tuscany. Everything here is harmony: the dark green of the cypresses contrasting with the silver sheen of the olive trees, the rolling hills outlined against the blue backdrop of the Apennines, the villas and the campaniles resting like flowers on the velvet carpet of the land.

The region of Tuscany — the Etruria of antiquity — lies within well-defined natural frontiers, between the mountainous horseshoe stretching from the Apuan Alps to the Apennines and the shores of the Tyrrhenian sea. It offers residents and visitors alike the pleasures of today — mountain walks, even skiing and the pleasures of the seaside all along the Tuscan Riviera while the hinterland holds the wonders of a host of cities which once vied with each other for supremacy in the arts.

In them the visitor can savor the charm of Tuscany, quite as much as in the major tourist centers, and particularly in spring and fall, in what Anatole France called "that delicate light which fondles beautiful shapes and nurtures noble thoughts".   P.L.

Above: a view of the hills in the Chianti region. Left: a narrow street in Florence, which has remained unchanged for centuries, the Via San Leonardo.

3

FLORENCE, THE CITY OF FLOWERS

The Romans were the founders of the city now known as Florence. Realizing the importance of a thoroughfare towards the Po plain, Ceasar in 59 B.C. ordered the establishment of a colony on the north bank of the Arno. The foundation is thought to have taken place in the spring, during the Floral Games, or *Ludi Florales*: hence the name *Florentia*, which was given to the city. Flora was the goddess of flowers and gardens, and the mother of spring in Roman mythology. Tuscan dialect turned the Latin *Florentia* into Fiorenza — a name which is to be found on Renaissance frescoes, and which was later shortened to Firenze.

Practically nothing now remains of the original Roman city, with its forum and four gates, which was situated on the site of the present Piazza della Repubblica. This square, which is perhaps better known to Florentines than to tourists, is bordered by some rather severe architecture. Outdoor cafes reach all the way into the middle of the piaza, where it is possible to stroll and relax without worrying too much about traffic which, as in other tourist spots, is limited to buses and taxis.

The Piazza della Repubblica is a meeting place and thoroughfare for busy people. In ancient times it was the Roman forum, where citizens debated the fate of the city. Under the arcades people still talk business or politics, or watch the well-dressed throngs go by. The men and women of Florence, who are renowned for their elegance, were described for us by André Suarès in his *Journey of the Condottiere*: "Florentines tend to be good-looking, refined and lively, with flashing eyes and quick gestures. They are also well-dressed, with neat clothes, shining shoes, and soft clean felt hats. Their speech has a throaty, singsong quality to it: there is certainly nothing bland about their mocking, caustic and full-bodied accent."

The ordinary people of Florence can be seen at work not far from the piazza, under the loggia of the Mercato Nuovo, with its abundance of small businesses. Knicknacks, cheap souvenirs, engravings and scarves are all on display in the midst of flowers, fruit, vegetables and the red watermelons which Florentines are so fond of.

The loggia of the Mercato Nuovo was built in the 16th century. According to tradition, visitors wishing to return eventuallly to Florence are supposed to rub the snout of the Porcellino, the bronze statue which stands guard near the Mercato Nuovo.

Apart from their esthetic pleasures, the markets are also a rich source of information. There are at a more popular level, particularly that of San Lorenzo, which is quite close to the central market. And, as one might expect in a city whose emblem is the red lily, there are flowers everywhere.

While one finds housewives in the markets, the cafés are the place to go to see people, from all segments of Florentine society. Like Rome or Paris, Florence has its own literary coffee houses. These are the *Michelangelo*, on Via Cavour, and *Giubbe Rossi*, which was patronized by Gide, Unamuno, Papini and the opponents of fascism, as well as Eugenio Montale, Elio Vittorini and others.

There is an abundance of restaurants, trattorias and pizzerias throughout Florence. From the Duomo to San Marco, from the station to the Oltrarno, visitors will find exactly the kind of eating place they need, and the variety of cooking of their choice, including a number of dishes which are specialties of Florence.

Above: views of the historical centre of Florence. Left: one of the quays along the Arno.

FLORENCE, BIRTH OF A CITY

Florence is a place to be stayed in, not merely visited. The sheer abundance of interesting monuments and the extraordinary treasures to be found in churches and museums alike could easily overwhelm any visitor who tried to 'do' Florence in a hurry, and could lead to severe cultural indigestion, in the midst of a feast of beauty. Like Venice, Florence is certainly not a dead town. Or even a museum. The centuries have been kind to it, so that it can now show us the past in a living context. The emotions we feel in certain other historic places, such as Carthage or Pompei, derive from memories which live on only in dust and ruins. But here the lifeblood of the city is still circulating around the monuments built by so many past generations, and the most delicate works of art — frescoes and paintings — make a symphony of color which is still as vivid as ever.

Florence has been shaped by history and art. This artistic gem was also the scene of numerous and bloody conflicts.

The Roman period was followed by the northern invaders whom Byzantium was powerless to stop: the Huns of Attila, who are mentioned by Dante, the Ostrogoths of Totila, and lastly the Lombards. It was not until the coming of the Carolingians that Florence began to emerge from several centuries of stagnation.

Having saved Europe from the Hungarian peril and triumphed over the princes, Emperor Otto was crowned Emperor of the West by Pope John XII. However, the title which was conferred on him was the source, almost immediately, of a conflict of authority, both spiritual and temporal, which was to dominate the entire history of the peninsula for almost three centuries.

It was not until 1183, after the comprehensive peace treaty signed by Pope Lucius III and Frederick Barbarossa that the independence of Florence was assured. The town was then controlled by a college of consuls, whose term of office was renewable every two months, and who were chosen from among the nobility as well as the general population, or rather the middle classes. Commerce was already the cornerstone of the town's life, bringing it its wealth, power and prestige.

Seen from any of several vantage points, Florence is an imposing sight, with its graceful domes and towers. One's eye is first caught by two pairs of structures, which stand like beacons overlooking the city: the campanile and dome of Santa Maria del Fiore, and the two towers of the Palazzo Vecchio and the Bargello. They represent the city's religious and civic aspects, in a mutually complementary rather than conflicting relationship. Indeed, both were from time to time enmeshed in each other's passions and moments of high drama.

These two architectural clusters also reflect the dual nature of Florence's destiny: beauty mingled with horror, the two contradictory faces of its past. In fact the whole history of the city is recorded within this perimeter between the Duomo and the Palazzo, where pedestrians now casually stroll.

Above: Florence in the 16th century. Right, top: the tower of the Palazzo Vecchio, 285 feet high, and the campanile of the Cathedral of Santa Maria dei Fiori, for which Giotto was responsible. Opposite: the Orsanmichele Church seen from outside.

SANTA MARIA DEL FIORE

In keeping with the Italian, and especially the Tuscan pattern, the cathedral of Florence consists of three independent elements: baptistery, campanile and dome.

The baptistery of St John, which was originally a cathedral, is the hub of the Christian town. It dates from somewhere between the 6th and the 11th centuries, and its design, which is so similar to that of the Pantheon in Rome, clearly shows the influence of Antiquity. Its octagonal shape imparts a closed mood, a secret majesty further ennobled by the mosaics of the cupola.

The glory of the baptistery owes more, however, to the exterior, with its harmonious marbles and particularly the gilded bronze panels of its three doors. They were made between 1330 and 1452, the first by Andrea Pisano and the rest by Ghiberti. From one century to the next, the craft of the sculptor had passed from the Middle Ages to the Renaissance, with the proliferation of its imagination and its symbols.

The elegant simplicity of the baptistery of St John contrasts with the façade of Santa Maria del Fiore, which was left unfinished for many years, repeatedly remodeled and eventually decorated late in the 19th century with a profusion of motifs, niches and pediments.

As soon as we pass through the door, which is thought to have been designed by Lorenzo the Magnificent, we find ourselves facing the massive and imposing nave. Santa Maria del Fiore is the biggest church in Italy, and also one of the most severe, one whose starkness is in sharp contrast with its wealth of exterior decoration. It is a meeting place rather than a house of prayer: a closed place, heavily laden with history. One can imagine Giuliano de Medici breathing his last, as he lay dying from the assassins' daggers, while Lorenzo fled from the choir to the sacristy; or Savonarola terrorizing and dominating the crowds which were

packed into the huge church. The large frescoes of mounted *condottiere* which adorn the walls also emphazize the grimness of Santa Maria del Fiore, whose name is such a misleading guide as to its true character. If Mary is present here at all, it is the Mary of Sorrows, who, with Mary Magdalen and Nicodemus holds the dead body of Christ in the admirable *Pieta* in the transept, which, like so many of his other works, Michelangelo was unable to complete.

The sole justification for the campanile is its nobility and its beauty. The actual purpose for which it was commissioned was to ensure that it would "surpass in magnificence, in height and in perfection whatever the Romans and the Greeks might have done in this king of architecture." This task was entrusted to Giotto. He drew up the plans in 1334, but died two years later; and, as in the case of the dome, his work was continued by Andrea Pisano and Francesco Talenti. The campanile is a geometric symphony of white Carrara marble, green Prato marble and pink Maremma marble, highlighted by sculptural variations: Pisano's low reliefs, executed, it is generally believed, from Giotto's drawings. Mythological scenes, allegories and symbols, peasants at work in the fields, the rhythm of the seasons... The niches were once adorned with statues by Donatelli, which can now be seen in the Museo dell'Opera del Duomo.

Left: the magnificent doors of the Baptistery of the Cathedral by S. Giovanni, and an overall view of the Baptistery, taken from the top of the Campanile. This page: view looking down on the Cathedral from the Campanile, and a detail of the Baptistery.

These two pages: details of the Cathedral: the main door (above), the façade in polychrome marble, the chancel (below) and the huge cupola, by the great architect Brunelleschi.

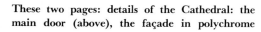

Above: an unusual glimpse of the Cathedral from one of the narrow streets around it. **Right, top:** looking down on a little street leading into the Square of the Seigniory, and the Loggia of the New Market. **Opposite:** one of the sides of the Square of the Seigniory.

12

THE PALAZZO VECCHIO
AND THE LOGGIA DEI LANZI

Between the two squares, which are linked by the Via Calzaioli, the association between the religious and the civic is represented by a monumental cubic structure. Orsanmichele originally belonged to the municipality before being transferred to the Church. Its dual allegiance is reflected in the sculptures which decorate its four faces: they are the patron saints of the guilds, the famous *Arti* which controlled the destiny of the city. They were carved in stone by the finest artists of the *Quattrocento*: Ghiberti, Donatello, Verrochio, In the interior, a tabernacle by Andrea Orcagna (14th century) used to house a miraculous image of the Virgin which was burnt and later replaced. This lavish and extravagantly Gothic work is quite out of proportion with the monument in which it is situated.

After the outbreak of the plague in 1348, the loggia which served as the base for this imposing wheat granary was dedicated to the Virgin.

The Palazzo Vecchio stands proudly on one corner of the Piazza della Signoria. The rigorous design of this building, the great size of its tow and the dignity of its windows and battlemen convey a true impression of Florence in its prim For nearly seven centuries the palace witnessed the major events of Florentine history. In 14 Archbishop Salviati and a handful of conspirate in the pay of the Pazzis were hanged from t windows of the Palazzo. In 1492 Savonarola car to power there, only to be burned alive, five yea later, in the middle of the square where, one ye earlier, the dreaded monk had tossed onto t flames a pile of vain objects such as books, *obj d'art*, and pictures which he found to be licentiou During the 15th and 16th centuries the Piaz della Signoria was often the scene of pub festivities, tournaments and games of *calcio* —

Left: the Palazzo Vecchio. Below: a coachman front of the entrance to the palace. Below: th statues in the square and the passage linking th Palazzo Vecchio and the Uffizi Gallery. Right: th famous motifs with the arms of the towns Tuscany, which adorn the top of the Palaz Vecchio, the fronton over the entrance, and th hall of the "Five Hundred", built by Pallaiolo.

REX REGVM ET
DOMINVS
DOMINANTIVM

spectacle which still takes place today, in Renai
sance costumes.

The sheer size of this building is even bette
conveyed by the huge Grand Council Hall, th
monumental stairways and the stately courtyard
which is so cool in summer! The charming *Chi*
with Dolphin, by Verrochio, which adorns th
fountain, strikes a contrasting note in such
majestic setting, just as the *Studiolo*, where Fran
cesco I de Medici locked up his treasures, is in stal
contrast with the lavish apartments of Leo X, th
second Medici pope.

Like most of the squares in Florence, the Piazz
della Signoria is attractive not because of the kin
of splendid, orderly layout of the squares of Rom
or Paris, but precisely on account of its diversit
and lack of balance.

The elegant arches of the Loggia dei Lanz
opposite the Palazzo Vecchio, house an open-a
museum. The loggia was built in 1380 as
guardroom for the Swiss lancers of Duke Cosimo
— whence its name. It contains some famou
sculptures, both originals and copies, beneath th
towering and haughty figure of *Perseus*, by Benv
nuto Cellini. In front of the entrance to the palazz
there is a copy of Michelangelo's *David*, and
fountain in which nymphs and satyrs dispo
themselves below the flabby hulk of a Neptur
known jokingly as *Il Biancone* — the 'big white one
The equestrian statue of Cosimo I by Jean Bologn
a short distance further along, was Florence
tribute to the first Grand-Duke of Tuscany (151
1574), who tried to restore the city's prestige, on th
return of the Medicis.

Passengers still alight from horse-drawn cabs i
the more attractive setting of the Piazza dell
Signoria. On that same square, opposite the augu
palazzo, serious chocolate drinkers congregate o
the terrace of Chez Rivoire!

Above: View of the Tower of the Palazzo Vecchi
from the interior courtyard, the statue of Perse
by Cellini, showing the head of Medusa, in fro
of the Loggia della Signoria, built at the end of th
14th century. Below: general view of the Loggi
and Neptune's Fountain. Right: a vista of th
Square of the Signoria, with the equestrian statu
of Cosimo I of the Medicis, the colossal statue
Neptune overshadowing the fountain, and a vie
looking down on the Piazza.

FROM THE BADIA TO THE BARGELLO

Quite close to the Palazzo Vecchio, on the Piazza San Firenze, we come to two other beacons of the city: the belltower of the Badia and the crenellated tower of the Bargello. The former abbey of La Badia, which dates from the year 1000, contains one of the most charming works of Filippino Lippi, The *Apparition of the Virgin to St Bernard*. And the church itself, somewhat neglected by the tourists, is a haven of peace and quiet.

Just over the road is the Bargello, the former seat of the podesta, founded in the 13th century, which now houses the national museum of Tuscan sculpture. There cannot be a city anywhere else in the world where this art form is as prominent as it is here. From Donatello to Michelangelo, from Verrochio to Jean Bologne, the great masters of sculpture have decorated its piazzas and adorned its palaces. Here they are present in works embodying the Bible and mythology, legend and history: *David* by Donatello, *Bacchus* by Michelangelo, *Ganymede* by Cellini... And the terra cottas of the Della Robbia family, together with low reliefs, ivories, tapestries and jewelry make up a dazzling treasury of art.

Here again the masterpieces of art conceal the horrors of history. The Bargello, which was built for the podesta and named after him, was also a prison and the residence of the chief of police. Savonarola spent his last night before his execution in its chapel. The Bargello had its torture chamber; until the 18th century a scaffold adorned with sculpted coats-of-arms stood in the middle of the courtyard. This gaunt building, quite as much as the Palazzo Vecchio, brings to mind he tragic face of the great centuries of Florentine history.

On either side of the axis which runs from the Duomo to the Palazzo Vecchio, now much frequented by tourists, particularly around the Bargello, we come to a network of narrow streets whose tall dwellings give an idea of what medieval Florence must have looked like. The Casa Cante is merely a reconstruction, in honor of the poet's memory, which dates from the beginning of the century. Yet this is the part of town where he was born, and the small nearby church of Santa Margherita was under the patronage of the Portinaris, the family of Beatrice, the young Florentine girl who inspired the poems of *Vita Nuova*. After her death at the age of twenty-four, in 1290, this adolescent love became for Dante an idealized image of womanhood; and in his major work, *The Divine Comedy* it was the symbol of Christian thinking, juxtaposed to Virgil, the symbol of the culture of Antiquity.

Born in 1265 in a distinguished Florentine family, Dante Alighieri fought on the side of the Guelphs, was elected to the Council of the Commune and sought a reconciliation between the Blacks and the Whites in the Guelph party. After the defeat of the Whites, the poet was doomed to exile. He died in 1321 at Ravenna, where his remains now lie, far from the city which he had both loved and cursed.

Left: a hall and a room in the Davanzati Palace. Right: view of the Bargello and of the superb campanile of the Church of the Badia, and a plate reminding the visitor of the places in Florence associated with Dante.

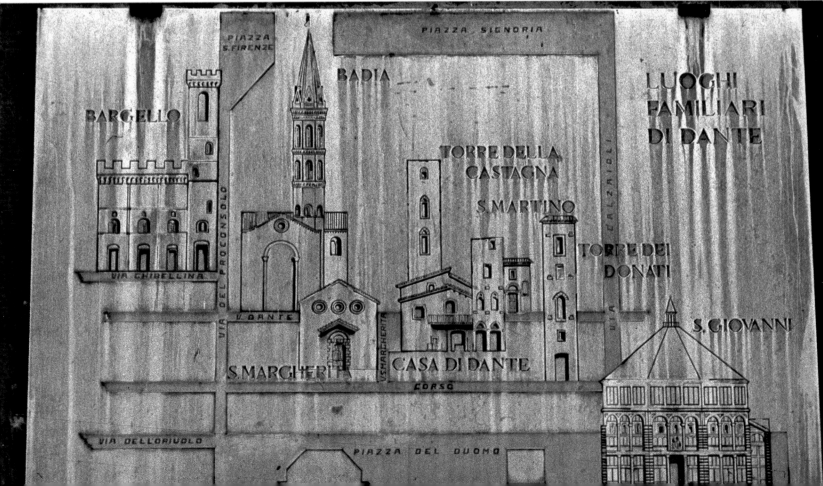

LUOGHI FAMILIARI DI DANTE

BARGELLO

PIAZZA S.FIRENZE

BADIA

PIAZZA SIGNORIA

TORRE DELLA CASTAGNA

S.MARTINO

TORRE DEI DONATI

VIA GHIBELLINA

VIA DEL PROCONSOLO

V.DANTE

VIA S.MARGHERITA

S.MARGHERITA

CASA DI DANTE

CORSO

VIA CALZAIOLI

S.GIOVANNI

VIA DELL'ORIUOLO

PIAZZA DEL DUOMO

THE FLORENCE OF THE MEDICIS

North of the Piazza del Duomo, Via Martelli takes us towards Via Cavour, formerly known as Via Larga because it was the first road which, unlike the narrow streets of the Middle Ages, was broad and straight. It was built by Cosimo the Elder, founder of the Medici dynasty, who chose it as the site for his palace.

Michelozzo began construction in 1444, using a plan which was to inspire the whole of Florentine architecture. The result was a square palace, closed to the outside world, with an inner courtyard adorned with sculptures and a garden. It was inhabited by the Medici family until 1540. During the time of Lorenzo the Magnificent it was the setting for a brilliant court at which artists, poets and scholars were received. Its visitors included kings and princes such as Charles VIII of France, and Emperor Charles V.

With the decline of the Medicis the palace was sold to the Riccardis for 287,000 pounds. The new owners made many profound alterations and gave the palace their name. All that now remains of the 15th-century structure is the private chapel, which is particularly worthy of attention as it contains the fresco by Benozzo Gozzoli entitled *The Procession of the Magi on their Way to Bethlehem.*

Today the Palazzo Riccardi houses the Prefecture, but it is possible to visit the Luca Giordano room, which has a ceiling mural of the *Apotheosis of the Second Dynasty of the Medicis* in keeping with the Baroque exuberance of the decor of this gallery, which dates from 1670.

The most illustrious members of the family lie buried in the sacristies of San Lorenzo, not far from the palace in which they lived their triumphant

lives — where Giovanni, the future Pope Leo X, and Catherine, the future Queen of France, spent their childhood. More than anywhere else therefore, this is the Florence of the Medicis.

San Lorenzo was their parish church, in the midst of a working-class district filled with that *popolo minuto* on which Cosimo the Elder was to base his power. Before him, Giovanni de Bicci had

Left: statue in the courtyard of the Medici Palace, and a view of the interior of its chapel. Above: the Church of San Lorenzo, built by Brunelleschi. Right: the splendour of the Princes' Chapel, at San Lorenzo's.

commissioned Brunelleschi to rebuild the original church in a manner befitting his ambitions. San Lorenzo, a huge building with three naves, Corinthian columns and semi-circular arches, contains works by Donatello – two bronze-paneled pulpits – and his tomb. The sculptures and reliefs adorning Brunelleschi's Old Sacristy are also his. Verrochio made some of the sarcophagi which contain the remains of several members of the family.

An even more rewarding visit can be made to the New Sacristy, or Medici Chapel, built by Michelangelo, and which houses the tombs of Giuliano, Duke of Nemours, and Lorenzo, Duke of Urbino. Michelangelo sculpted four allegorical figures for these tombs: *Day, Night, Dawn* and *Dusk*, which are widely regarded as some of his finest masterpieces. Lorenzo the Magnificent and his brother Giuliano, the victims of the Pazzi conspiracy, lie in another tomb for which Michelangelo was able to complete only the *Madonna and Child* and which was never finished.

The tombs of some other Medicis are located in the Chapel of the Princes, the decor of which is breathtakingly rich. The fine clositer next to the church leads to the Biblioteca Laurenziana (Laurentian Library), which was also built by Michelangelo, and contains many priceless manuscripts and incunabila. And we find another Medici, Giovanni delle Bande Nere, in the form of a statue in front of the uncompleted façade of San Lorenzo: indeed the *condottiere* seems to be standing guard outside the final restingplace of his ancestors.

THE TREASURES OF FLORENTINE ART

It is significant that the guilds which, from the Middle Ages onwards, built the prosperity of Florence, were known in those days as the *Arti* — literally, the Arts. They covered all activities. There was the art of wool, the art of money-changing, the art of cloth-making and even that of grocery! The meaning of the term changed over the centuries, but its origin seems to suggest that the art of Florence is more than one form of its activity: instead, it is all of that activity — in other words, life itself.

Cimabue (1240-1302) and particularly his pupil Giotto (1266-1337) were men of the Middle Ages. They were the heirs of Byzantium, but their lives were not based on that inheritance. The saints of Christianity and the gods of Greece were both to appear in the works of sculptors and fresco painters. Marsilio Ficino, who was a religious and a philosopher, sought to unite Platonic thought and Christian doctrine. Early in the 15th century — the *Quattrocento* — there began that great outpouring of creativity which was to make Florence the largest living museum which has ever been assembled in such a small space.

The buildings of the Uffizi, which when seen from the Arno provide such a superb frame for one's view of the Palazzo Vecchio, were the result of an initiative of Cosimo I, who intended it to accommodate the city's offices *(uffizi)* and archives. The works of art acquired by the Medici family were also included, and in this way the collections of the present museum were gradually built up.

First the visitor is impressed by the *Virgins in Majesty* of Cimabue and Giotto, which still bear the imprint of the Byzantine hieratic style. After Masaccio, who is represented by a *Madonna*, the Renaissance fully asserts itself with the large canvas by Paolo Uccello (1397-1475), *The Battle of San Romano.*

Fra Angelico (1387-1455) was certainly the last mystic in Italian art. Fra Filippo Lippi (1406-1469) was a monk like Angelico, but he was hardly of an ascetic nature. He abducted the nun who posed for his *Virgins* and gave her a child, Filippino Lippi, a future pupil of Botticelli who, in turn, had been a pupil of Filippo Lippi. These three painters brought to pictures of the Virgin a youthful freshness, more secular than sacred, which makes them more human, more moving and closer to us. This delicacy of craftsmanship and bittersweet tenderness reached their peak with Sandro Botticelli (1445-1510), the most secret painter of the Florentine school and, accordingly, one of the most endearing. The entire room devoted to his works at the Uffizi is a dazzling sight. It is dominated by two of his most famous masterpieces: *The Birth of Venus*, an admirable figure whose languid charm has never been surpassed, and *The Spring.*

When Botticelli was sinking into a religious crisis and preparing his own purgatory, two other Tuscans — Leonardo da Vinci (1452-1519) and Michelangelo (1475-1564) — were just about to reach the height of their powers. The works of theirs which can be seen at the Uffizi date from their youth: *The Annunciation*, which Leonardo painted while he was a pupil in the studio of Verrochio, and the unfinished *Adoration of the Magi.*

The works contained within these walls are so enchanting that one cannot be content to merely stroll through the halls of the Uffizi on a single visit: it is essential to come back, to experience new thrills among the masters of the late *Cinquecento*, and the foreign schools of painting which are so brilliantly represented here.

Left: the Uffizi Gallery and one of the numerous rooms, with works by Giotto and Cimabue. Right: example of a richly-decorated ceiling in the palace and one of the corridors of the famous gallery.

Above and right: the great men of Florence; these statues decorate the Uffizi Gallery. Middle: detail of a ceiling.

Below and right: corridors of the vast museum and the portrait of Cosimos of the Medicis, the "enlightened despot".

BENVENUTO CELLINI

GIOVANNI BOCCACCIO

GIOTTO

GALILEO GALILEI

GUIDO ARETINO

LEONARDO DA VINCI

FRANCESCO PETRARCA

DANTE ALLIGHIERI

NICCOLÒ MACCHIAVELLI

The palaces of the great Florentine families — Davanzati, Rucellai, Antinoni, Strozzi — stand on the right bank of the Arno, beyond the Piazza della Signoria, their massive embossed façades adding a somewhat forbidding air to their grandeur. There are some interesting churches on the streets which lie between them: San Apostoli, a Romanesque basilica with three naves, and Santa Trinita, with its Baroque façade and frescoes by Ghirlandaio. The church of Ognissanti (founded 1256), which is situated a short distance further on, overlooking the Arno, also has a fine Baroque façade dating from 1638. One of its chapels is dedicated to the Vespucci family, one of whose sons, the navigator Amerigo, gave his name to the New World. Sandro Botticelli and Caroline Bonaparte are buried here. A precious relic is on display at the Ognissanti church: the cloak worn by St Francis of Assisi at Alverna when he received the stigmata. In the nearby cloister there are some frescoes which tell his story, and also a large and rightly famous *Last Supper* by Ghirlandaio, which is thought to have

been the inspiration for the painting which Leonardo later produced for the Convento della Grazie in Milan.

The Old Bridge deserves its name, as there is none older than it in Florence. The present structure dates from the 14th century, but there had previously been a bridge at the same site ever since Roman times. And it already had its own history. On Easter Sunday 1215 a young nobleman named Buondelmonte was assassinated for his failure to marry the daughter of the Amidei family, as he was bound to do by contract. This may not have seemed a very portentous event at the time, though it did set in motion the centuries-long struggle between Guelphs and Ghibellines.

Above: dusk on the Arno and the Ponte Vecchio, from the Piazzale Michelangelo. Left: the corridor linking the Uffizi Gallery to the Ponte Vecchio. Right: view looking down on the Ponte Vecchio, the most famous bridge in the world.

Disastrous floods in 1333 swept away the original bridge. It was replaced by a more solid structure which Cosimo I, in an inspired move, had reserved thereafter for goldsmiths and jewelers — and they are still there today. Living quarters for the merchants are located behind the double row of shops, overhanging the river — a delightful piece of whimsical architecture. The middle of the bridge is open in the form of a loggia, decorated with a bust of Benvenuto Cellini, from which there is a captivating view of both banks of the Arno and the neighboring bridges.

In spring, particularly, when the sun sets along the axis of the river, the Tuscan sky, which is so subtle and fine, reflects the most delicate tones in its waters.

The next bridge downstream, the Ponte Trinita, was built by Ammanati, between 1566 and 1569. Plays were also performed here. And, according to legend, it was here that Dante met Beatrice. The bridge was very faithfully rebuilt in 1957, and is now once again adorned with the statues of the seasons. And the unpredictable Arno, with its potential for disastrous floods, flows on.

By day or by night, visitors enjoy strolling across the bridge, admiring the wares for sale in the little shops, which have been reserved since the time of Cosimos I for goldsmiths and jewellers. Following pages: the bridge from another angle, divided in the middle by a loggia.

FROM SANTA MARIA NOVELLA TO SANTA CROCE

These two basilicas are separated by the entire old town. They stand like milestones at either end. Santa Maria Novella is the church of the Dominicans and Santa Croce that of the Franciscans. They seem to be curiously in harmony with each other, as if they were the two poles of the religious orders which were to leave such a profound imprint on later centuries.

Dominicans and Franciscans stand guard at the gates of the city, roughly halfway from Santa Maria del Fiore — an architectural triptych symbolizing the faith of Florence.

Santa Maria Novella is, first of all, a façade, which is doubtless the most graceful in the city. Starting from a Romano-Gothic base, it rises to a portal enriched with Renaissance motifs paid for by the Rucellai family.

Though work began in 1278 it remained for many years unfinished, and was not completed until 1470, from designs by Alberti.

It has a tall slender nave and two lateral naves lined by the chapels of the Rucellai, Strozzi, Gaddi and other notable families. A wooden crucifix by Brunelleschi, a fresco by Masaccio, and, in particular, the fine series of frescoes painted by Domenico Ghirlandaio between 1485 and 1490 in the high altar chapel are the most interesting works of art in Santa Maria Novella.

By their nobility of composition, enchanting poses and rich colors, Ghirlandaio's extraordinary frescoes mark him out clearly as one of the masters of his time.

The green cloister contains the Spanish Chapel, whose walls are entirely covered with frescoes by Andreas di Buonaiuto (1355).

Ornamental ponds and obelisks standing on bronze turtles decorate the lawns which stretch away in front of the church Santa Maria. The obelisks were used as goals in the chariot races which took place from the 16th to the 19th centuries.

The Piazza Santa Croce, at the other end of town, is situated in front of the Franciscan church. Children play ball in the center of the square between the fine façades — some of which have frescoes painted on them — of 16th-century houses.

Early in the 13th century the small craftsmen of the neighborhood — located outside the city walls — used to come to listen to the Franciscan friars in a small church dedicated to the Holy Cross. Arnolfo di Cambio was commissioned to replace it in the 13th century, and made this building the biggest of the Franciscan churches.

As soon as the visitor enters he is struck by the great size and majesty of the nave. Beneath a polychrome wood ceiling, on either side of the ogival arcades, there are rows of funerary monuments which make Santa Croce the Pantheon of Florence. Michelangelo, Ghiberti, Machiavelli and Galileo are all buried there, in emphatically allegorical tombs, which are mostly the work of Vasari. A cenotaph evokes the memory of Dante, whose remains never left Ravenna, which refused to part with them.

Giotto is to Santa Croce what Ghirlandaio is to Santa Maria Novella. His work has a sense of grandeur, and a sort of purity which entitle him to a special place in the history of painting, and not merely that of his own time. Giotto (1266-1337) was the pupil of Cimabue. Three years before his death he was put in charge of the artwork of Florence.

In Santa Croce we also find the work of Brunelleschi, in the Pazzi Chapel, next to the

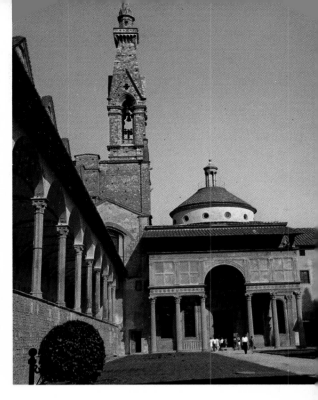

basilica, at the end of the cloister. This triumph of refinement and balance is adorned with medallions by Donatello and Luca Della Robbia.

Left: views of the façade, of the Campanile, of the cloisters and of the interior of the Church of Santa Maria Novella, which dates back to the 13th century. Above: the church and the cloisters of Santa Croce. Below: two altars of this fine church.

THE DISTRICT OF SAN SPIRITO

At the south end of the Ponte Vecchio a small and lively intersection leads into the Oltrarno. There are a number of roads which provide access, and one should take them in succession in order to discover the various aspects of this south side of Florence.

To the right, the Borgo San Jacopo leads to the Piazza San Spirito, which is occupied in its center by a garden with a fountain and statue, and also by the local market and the church of the same name. The architect was Brunelleschi, but construction was carried out by his pupil Manetti. A campanile was added in the 16th century, but the façade was not completed. San Spirito is a basilica with the naves and thirty-six columns of grey stone. It contains artworks from different periods. The former monastery near the church now houses the fine collection of sculptures of the Romano Foundation.

Though it started life as a poor neighborhood, this area of often narrow streets became enriched in the 16th century with the palaces of members of the Grand Duke's court in the Palazzo Pitti. This astonishing mixture of ancient houses and princely dwellings will prove most rewarding to an inquisitive tourist. He will discover here and there an emblazoned doorway, bronze knockers on sculpted doors, or a Baroque fountain in the courtyard of a palace.

San Spirito is the craftsmen's neighborhood. They can still be seen in their stalls and shops. This is a tradition which is very much part of the city's economy, and which its practitioners passionately defend, dreading as they must the impersonal nature of much of today's commerce.

Santa Maria del Carmine is the other pole of the Oltrarno district. Devotion to the Virgin Mary prompted the Carmelites to build a church here in the 13th century. In 1771 it was destroyed by fire. Only the façade, now stripped of all ornamentation, and a few chapels in the transept managed to survive. The central nave was rebuilt. Fortunately, the Brancacci chapel had been preserved. Built with funds generously contributed by a 15th-century silk merchant, it represents an important phase in the history of painting, on account of the frescoes painted in it by Tommaso, a young pupil of Masolino, whose casual dress earned him the nickname Masaccio. At the time, he was twenty-five years old: he worked for one year on the chapel and then left for Rome, where he died in 1428, at the age of twenty-seven, without ever realizing his full potential.

Like Donatello in sculpture, Masaccio brought real life into art. One only has to look at his *Adam and Eve driven from Paradise*, and witness the reality of the subjects' grief, in order to understand that, with Masaccio, painting became imbued with the spirit of humanism.

Sixty years later, Filippino Lippi completed some of these frescoes. But the course of art had been changed, and the change was due to Masaccio.

The Borgo San Frediano, with the church of the same name, situated beyond the Piazza del Carmine, belongs to the same picturesque neighborhood. It is occasionally said to have a bad reputation! The Lungarno Soderini and the Ponte della Vittoria lead us back to the right bank at the Piazza Vittorio-Emmanuele, an important intersection leading to the Cascine, a complex of gardens with a hippodrome, sports fields, tennis courts and broad promenades.

Left: detail of the interior of a chapel of the Church of the Carmine, adorned with frescoes by Masaccio. Above: the facade of the Excelsior Grand Hotel, on the banks of the Arno. Right: a view of the house of Ghiberti. Bottom: Michelangelo's house and a plate on the house where Galileo lived, the Renaissance church of the *Santo Spirito*.

FROM SAN MARCO TO THE ANNUNZIATA

The northern districts of Florence also have their sacred core, which stretches from San Marco to the Annunziata. The church of San Marco, originally designed by Michelozzo, was remodeled by Jean Bologne in the 15th century, in a Baroque style. The façade is of the 18th century. The interior houses the mortal remains of two great thinkers of the period: Agnolo Poliziano and Pico della Mirandola, who was noted for his precocious genius.

Fra Angelico, a monk from Fiesole, was instructed by the prior to paint frescoes on the friars' cells. Working with a few pupils, he painted his visions of celestial glory, from the Annunciation to the Transfiguration. His pictures of Christ are charged with symbols.

Less than forty years later, another monk, a native of Ferrare, was appointed prior of San Marco. His name was Girolamo Savonarola. His face thin and drawn, his eyes blazing, he vehemently hurled his anathemas at the joyous city where Lorenzo the Magnificent reigned supreme. Within no time at all, the cowed multitudes awaited in fear and trembling the punishments with which he threatened the city.

Savonarola did not spare the church. Excommunicated for rebellion against the pope, he was gradually abandoned by the very people who had brought him to power. He was arrested, hanged

and burnt, afer what is described on a plaque still visible on the Piazza della Signoria as an "iniquitous trial". Savonarola's cell contains portraits and some mementoes of his meteoric passage through the history of Florence.

Two hundred yards from the Piazza San Marco we come to another square: Santissima Annunziata, bordered on three sides by elegant porticoes which make it one of the most charming squares in Florence. The oldest of these buildings is the Ospedale degli Innocenti (Home for Lost Children): the portico was designed by Brunelleschi and decorated with terra cotta medallions by Andrea della Robbia (1463) depicting swaddled infants.

The church, which occupies another corner of the square, was originally a modest sanctuary of the Confraternity of St Lawrence, which was dedicated to the Virgin Mary. The richly adorned Baroque interior is in sharp contrast with the austerity of the other churches in Florence. The nave belonging to the period in which it was originally built disappears, in fact, beneath the decorative work of the 17th and 18th centuries. Chapels and funerary

monuments — those of several Medicis and of Andrea del Sarto — were erected there. The Chiostri dei Morti, which adjoins the church, contains some other tombs, in particular that of Benvenuto Cellini.

The third portico is that of the Confraternity which was originally associated with the church.

The visitor should certainly pay a visit to the nearby Museo dell'Accademia, where Michelangelo reigns triumphant, with the large figures he sketched for the tomb of Julius II. They seem to spring from the still shapeless marble, and convey a rare impression of creative power in action. The original of the prodigious *David*, of which copies can be seen in the Piazza della Signoria and the Piazzale Michelangelo, is located in a rotunda.

Left: the library of St. Mark's monastery, and the cloisters. It is here that one can admire the works of Fra Angelico. Above and below: St. Mark's Church and the original of the famous *David* by Michelangelo, at the *Accademia* Gallery.

THE PALAZZO PITTI AND THE BOBOLI GARDENS

Via Guicciardini, on the other side of the Ponte Vecchio, leads into the Piazza Pitti. The house where Machiavelli lived and died is at no. 16 on the via, and the one in which Dostoievski stayed is a little further on, opposite the palace. The Palazzo Pitti towers over the square like a fortress.

It was begun in 1458 from the plans drawn up by Brunelleschi for Luca Pitti, a rich banker who was implicated, ten years later, in a conspiracy against Cosimo the Elder's son, Piero il Gottoso, and thus compelled to give up his palace. Cosimo I, the first Grand-Duke of Tuscany, set up his court there, and it was there that Maria de Medici spent her youth.

The palace was enlarged — with the addition of two wings — in the 17th and 18th centuries. During the reign of Gian Gastone de Medici (1671-1737), it became, in the words of the historian P. Antonetti, a "genuine brothel"! Anna Maria Luisa (1667-1743), the last of the Medicis, bequeathed the family collections to the Tuscan state.

It is those collections which, even more than its interior and its gardens, make up the wealth of the Palazzo Pitti. The Galleria Palatina contains 500 paintings, mainly from the 16th century, and not only of Florentine art, but also of the Roman, Venetian, Spanish and Flemish schools. Raphael, Andrea del Sarto, Titian, Tintoretto, Velasquez and Rubens are the main attractions of the gallery.

The Museo degli Argenti is also well worth seeing, with ten rooms full of mementoes (vases,

dishes, cameos, porcelain, embroideries, etc.), either presented as gifts by the Medicis or commissioned by them. The sumptuous character of the royal apartments matches the display of these priceless treasures.

The Palazzo Pitti stands on the lower slopes of the hill. To the rear it continues in the form of the Boboli Gardens, started in 1549 by Tribolo at the request of Cosimo I. These gardens in the Italian style are laid out around a central axis decorated with statues in the manner of Antiquity, with groves, grottoes and fountains, striking a nice balance between intellectual rigor and natural fantasy.

The Boboli Gardens stretch as far as the Porta Romana in the west and eastwards to the Belvedere Fort, from the terraces from which there are fine views of Florence.

In order to get there, however, one has to return to the Ponte Vecchio and make one's way up the Via della Costa San Giorgio, where Galileo's house is situated (no. 14). The Via di Belvedere, running between old walls and olive groves, leads to the Piazzale Michelangelo.

Beyond the severe contours of the Palazzo Pitti, the Boboli Gardens, the façade of San Miniato and the Belvedere Fort, the orchards and cypresses, at the very gates of the city, are a prelude to the Tuscan landscapes of the interior.

Above: the Boboli Gardens and the Pizzi Palace dominating Florence. Bottom: the main façade of the palace. Right: pools, statues and one of the paths through the Gardens.

FROM SAN MINIATO TO FIESOLE: A HILLY SETTING

The Piazzale Michelangelo is a broad platform on which, in 1875, a group of bronze casts of the artist's main Florentine works was erected.

From the terrace there is a panoramic view of the entire city with its domes, towers and the fine ochre tint of its roofs. Down below are the Arno and its bridges, and the plain from Florence to Pistoia. Beyond that, the outlines of the hills recede as far as

Above and left: The church of *San Miniato al Monte,* a magnificent 12th-century building in green and white marble, on one of the hills surrounding the town. Right, top: the road leading to Fiesola, on another hill, and, opposite, a villa on the slopes of the same hill. Following pages: the façade of *San Miniato.*

the peaks of the Apennines in the bluish haze. Behind us there is a 16th-century loggia now turned into a café, and the little church of San Salvatore al Monte, which Michelangelo used to call his "sweet country girl". The marvelous façade of white and green marble was built in the 13th century. In the middle, a mosaic surrounded by the Madonna and St Miniato, in a style clearly influenced by Byzantium, emits flashes of gold in the setting sun.

The same harmony is discernible in the interior: three naves separated by arches decorated with geometric patterns, Renaissance chapels with terra cottas and sculptures and a polychrome wood ceiling.

The Viale dei Colli runs past orchards and gardens to the Via San Leonardo, a narrow, quiet road which winds its way between walled enclosu-

res in the shade of olive trees, cypresses and magnolias, and old villas with overhanging roofs. The house that Tchaikovsky lived in is readily identifiable because of its unusual balconies.

The beauty of Florence also lies in the charm of the Florentine countryside. The hills which rise on either side of the Arno valley make a harmoniously balanced landscape in which the presence of man — in his village and campaniles — fits unobtrusively into the verdant setting.

The origins of Fiesole can be traced back to the 6th century before Christ. However, its name first appears in history in 285 B.C., when the Etruscans were defeated by the Roman legions. Fiesole then bacame the Roman Faesulae. It was destroyed in 80 B.C., having mistakenly sided with Marius against Sylla.

The ruins which lie along the slopes of the

Mugnone valley date from this period. All that remains from Etruscan times is a gate and a number of segments of walls. But it is this Florentine town that the traveler enters when alighting from car or bus in the enormous and lively Piazza Mino da Fiesole, which is ringed by restaurants and trattorie, as well as by the Bishop's Palace and the Duomo.

However, the main attraction of Fiesole, in both archeological and scenic terms, is the ruins of the Roman theater, which were discovered in 1809. The theater, which was embellished by Claudius and Septimus Severus, us built in a semicircle overlooking the Mugnone valley and the hills of Mugello, the area in which the Medici family originated.

The monastery of San Francesco, at 1120 ft., higher up the hill against which the left part of th Roman theater is built. The view from the terrac embraces Florence and the Arno valley, as far a the distant Apennine peaks. The closed cloiste inside the monastery is blissfully peaceful. It is als possible to visit the cell where St Bernardino d Sienna once lived.

Fiesola. Left and below: the main square of th village, the little garden and the chapel c St. François monastery; the remains of a Roma arch. Right: Roman columns reconstructed in th excavations; below: the Pretorian Palace and th amphitheatre.

Poggio a Caiano, above the Ombrone stream of which Lorenzo and his friends were so fond, was another villa much cherished by the Medicis. It has a peristyle in the ancient manner, a vaulted ceiling adorned with an unfinished fresco by Filippino Lippi, and a long balustraded terrace overlooking the gardens.

Lastly, above the village of Settignano, Villa Gamberaia has a rock garden, and a terrace with pools framed by boxwoods and yew trees. The true art of living which is associated with Florence is best conveyed by these country houses.

The monks were, together with the Medicis, the principal moving force in the countryside around Florence, One of the finest religious houses in the region is situated a few miles from the city. It is the Charterhouse of Galuzzo, founded in 1342 by Nicolas Acciaiuoli, a Florentine friend of Petrarch and Boccaccio, and High Constable of the kingdom of Naples, where he had made his fortune.

Beyond the charterhouse we come to the village of Impruneta, where the famous fair, in honor of St Luke, is held every year in mid-October. A very interesting trip can be made to the Charterhouse of Vallombrosa, which was founded in the 11th century by St Jean Gualbert. The monastery played an essential role in the reform of the church and was, from 1035 to 1085, the center of a spiritual renewal in Florence. Now it houses a forestry school.

VILLAS AND CHARTERHOUSES

Villa Palmieri, right at the foot of the hill on which Fiesole is situated, brings to mind the Decameron. Boccaccio chose it as the setting in which a group of young men and women fleeing the plague which was then raging in Florence, told the stories which make up the collection.

The villas — the luxurious 'second homes' of the Florentine families of the city's golden age — are rich in memories, and contrast sharply, by virtue of their elegance and grace, with the more austere urban palaces.

While most of the villas are in the Renaissance style, some of them have much older origins. This is true, for instance, of Villa della Petraia, a former castle, complete with tower and sentinels' path, which was the scene of bloody clashes between Florentines and Pisans in the 14th century. At the end of the century, the castle was remodeled by Buontalenti for Ferdinand de Medici as a princely villa, with a garden and a grove of cypresses and other trees, The villa, which is admirably situated at the edge of the Florence plain, was further altered in the 19th century, and became the favorite residence of Victor-Emmanuel II, while Florence was the capital of Italy.

Not far from Villa della Petraia, Villa de Castello was bought in 1477 by the Medicis and embellished by Lorenzo the Magnificent. Beyond the avenue, with its border of chestnut trees, it comes into sight with its curious central keep and a terraced garden laid out by Tribolo in 1540.

Villa I Collazi, which is quite as old, is thought to have been built from Michelangelo's plans by Buondelmonti, in the second half of the 16th century. Its white façade stands on a hill and is surrounded by cypresses in front of which a spacious terrace offers a splendid view of the Chianti vineyards.

Above: the Carthusian monastery of Vallombrosa its cloisters and a view of its kitchens. Below: a plate on the villa where the famous English poet John Milton lived, and a view of the house. Right. The Medici villas at Poggio a Gaiano and Petraia and a manor house in the Florentine countryside Below: the house where Tchaikovsky lived and another where d'Annunzio lived.

ART IN THE CITIES OF TUSCANY

A constellation of art-rich cities sparkles all around Florence. Between the mountains and the sea, they offer the visitor the most astonishing array of architectural wonders, from primitive Etruscan to the splendors of the Renaissance, which make each town and village a life-size museum.

From Florence to Pisa, for those who prefer to leave the *autostrada,* there are two roads which pass either side of the Albano Mountains. The village of Vinci, set back against the foothills, was the birthplace of Leonardo da Vinci, in 1452. The museum and the library, which are so prized among scholars, are located in the old castle at the top of the village. The house in which the painter was born — now reconstructed — is adorned with a bust which gazes out over the surrounding country-side.

To the north of this small massif, the road to Pisa goes through three artistic cities : Prato, Pistoia and Lucca, and a well-known thermal spa, Montecatini Terme, where ailments of the liver and stomach are treated.

After leaving Florence, however, one should really go to Prato, which is practically in its suburbs. This is the birthplace of Filippino Lippi, Fra Bartolomeo and Malaparte, who wrote of it with humor and affection. The Piazza del Duomo was its church with a Gothic façade of white and green marble. The interior is graced by works of Della Robbia and the *Dancing Cupids* of Donatello. Nearby is the Piazza del Commune and its fountain of the child Bacchus in front of the town hall, and the Romanesque-Gothic Palazzo Pretorio, whose halls contain some fine works by Filippo Lippi, Filippino and Signorelli. And there are other churches, too, in fact more than one could possibly cover : San Domenico, with a Renaissance cloister and Baroque interior ; San Vicenzo e Caterina, in 18th century rococo ; and Santa Maria delle Carceri, clad in polychrome marble. Opposite the last of these stands the Castello dell'Imperatore, rebuilt in 1248 by Emperor Frederick II of Swabia, with massive towers and marble portals.

Pistoia, a bigger city and quite as rich, is a provincial and diocesan, seat which was a free commune in the 12th century, before becoming a Medici possession in 1530.

The Duomo was founded in the 5th century, and provides, in a 12th century restoration, a fine example of the Pisan-Romanesque style. The campanile has three floors of colonnaded galleries. The baptistery of green and white marble was the work of Andrea Pisano. The Piazza Communale (13th and 14th centuries), situated on the same square, has a portico of Gothic arcades, in contrast with the severity of the Palazzo del Podesta. The same graceful, elegant Pisan-Romanesque style can be seen in a number of other churches : San Andrea, San Giovanni Fuorcivitas, San Bartolomeo, San Pietro, San Francesco... A dazzlingly beautiful sight.

Top: the Piazza della Communa, at Prato. Left and above: the outside pulpit of the Cathedral and the Church of *San Pietro*. Below: delightful terra cotta decorations in color on the façade of the Hospital of Pistoia.

Pistoia. The campanile of the Cathedral (13th century). Above: flowers of colored straw, sold for the "Mostra dell'Orso", an annual festival of the town. Below: two pictures of this celebration.

LUCCA, CITY OF PRINCESSES

The ramparts built around the city in the 16th and 17th centuries are now a splendid promenade, with many vantage points overlooking an admirable urban landscape. The city inside the walls was built on the pattern of the Roman army camp from which it originated, before the Christian era. After passing through the gates, one enters a world of narrow streets, with wrought-iron grills over the windows, opening onto large squares which, in the evenings, remind one of the setting for a Fellini movie, particularly during the night-time procession, held each year, in honor of the Volto Santo (Holy Face), the sacred image which is stored in the treasury of the Duomo. According to legend, this miraculous crucifix was the work of Nicodemus — a statuette of Christ after the crucifixion. The face was said to have been designed by an angel.

History sometimes sounds just legend. The large Piazza Napoleone honors the memory of Elisa Bonaparte, the sister of the French emperor, who showed such great organizing skills that she came to be known as the Semiramis of Lucca.

Her sister, Pauline Bonaparte, the mad Princess Borghese, died in exile in a villa not far from Lucca, at Monte San Quirico.

The statue of Marie-Louise de Bourbon, in front of the Palazzo della Prefettura on the Piazza Napoleone, commemorates the institution of the duchy of Lucca, after the fall of Napoleon.

The Duomo is dedicated to St. Martin. Its sumptuous façade has three galleries of slender columns, supported by three arcades in the Pisan style. The low reliefs around the central porch relate the life of St. Martin and depict each of the months of the year. A crenellated campanile stands next to the Duomo, which is also worth visiting for the statues and funerary monuments which it contains.

The oratory of Santa Maria della Rosa, a short distance from the Piazza San Martin is an elegant, triple-nave structure in the Pisan Gothic style.

Other buildings worthy of the visitor's attention include the Palazzo Pretorio, with its 15th-and 16th-century arcades : the 12th-century church of San Michele, which has a 13th-century façade : the church of San Salvatore and Santa Maria Corteolandi, partly of the 13th century, with a Baroque façade ; the Romanesque church of San Frediano, Whose façade includes a Byzantine-Romanesque mosaic ; San Francesco, with a wealth of interesting tombstones ; and a number of others which testify to the importance of this town, which is the local archdiocesan seat.

The beautiful gardens of the Villa Reale de Marlia, five miles from Lucca, were laid out by Elisa Bonaparte, while those of the Villa Torrigiani were the work of Le Nôtre, who built them for the ambassador of Lucca to the Pontifical Court and the court of Louis XIV. The villa has had some distinguished guests, one of the most recent being Georges Pompidou, who stayed there in 1972 on the invitation of the Italian Government.

Lucca. This page: interior and façade of the Church of *San Frediano*; façade of the Church of *San Michele*. Right: the Market Place and a view of the ramparts; Liberty Gate; door and windows in a narrow old street.

ANCHIANO
CASA NATALE
DI
LEONARDO

ALONG THE ARNO VALLEY TOWARDS PISA

The natural route from from Florence to Pisa is that taken by the Arno, which is the quintessential Tuscan river, rising as it does in the Casentino and reaching the sea at Pisa. Once a trading port, this town now finds itself well inland, as the Ligurian Sea has receded over the centuries, causing it to lose much of its former importance. Both the highway and the railroad follow the course of the valley.

On the outskirts of Florence, past the industrial suburbs, the gently rolling landscape is very much in the image of the province : hills covered with vineyards and cypresses, and quaint hilltop villages, such as Lastra a Signa, its square belltower rising above the rooftops spread over the slope.

Left, top: the tiered gardens of the villa Garzoni at Collodi. Below: view of the ancient city of Vinci, where Leonard was born in 1452, a commemorative plate at the entrance to the house where he was born, and a detail of the ornamentation of one of its windows. Opposite and above: two different views of the Val d'Arno, near Incisa. Right: the Bandinella Tower, on the banks of the river.

The church of San Giovanni, in the village of Montelupo-Fiorentino, has a *Virgin with Child* attributed to Botticelli.

Empoli, a large farming center where glassware is also made, marks the beginning of the plain. The collegiate church of this lively town has an 11th-century Romanesque façade. Empoli also has a worthwhile museum of sacred art, containing marble and wooden sculptures, frescoes and paintings by Filippino Lippi, Taddeo Gaddi, Mino da Fiesole and other great artists of the Florentine school.

The highway and the railroad then go on to San Miniato-Basso, at the foot of San Miniato, a diocesan seat where the 1944 air raids killed sixty people in the Duomo, a 12th-century building which has now been restored. The ruins of La Rocca, where Frederick Barbarossa once lived, can be reached by a path to the left of the church.

From this point on, the Arno Valley opens out to form a broad plain of croplands, with the Tuscan Apennines, bluish in the warm haze, in the background. The road passes through farming villages, past houses with overhanging roofs in the midst of the orchards, as well as some small towns : Pontedera, at a crossroads ; Cascina, which has

kept its medieval fortifications and an oratory of the Knights of Rhodes (14th century), with frescoes and a polyptych. And then we reach Pisa, on a road which runs parallel to the river as it enters town.

Like Florence, Pisa was once the capital of a republic. It was also a trading port which rivalled Genoa and Venice, triumphed over the Saracens and then took Corsica, Sardinia and the Balearic Islands. Pisa reached the height of its prestige in the 12th and 13th centuries, when it had a school of architecture and a renowned university.

The major north-south roads through the town are separated by a web of narrow streets of tall

houses with twin stained-glass windows. The wharves all along the banks of the river, on the Lungarno, are lined with forbidding palaces, some of which have turned into movie theaters !

Standing alone on the waterfront, the exquisite chapel of Santa Maria della Spina is a gem of the 14th century, carved by the goldsmiths of the Pisano school. On the other side of the Arno is the National Museum, which contains works of that dynasty of sculptors which dominated the art of the entire region, and also a polyptych by Simone Martini. Lastly, on the road leading to the Duomo, we come to the Piazza dei Cavalieri, which, with its majestic palace, has the severe grandeur of the Order of the Knights of St Stephen, which was founded by Cosimo I.

Pisa. Left: the houses along the quayside of the Arno, and the façade of the Palace "dei Cavalieri", in the square of the same name, extravagantly decorated by Vasari. Right: another view of this square, the historical centre of the town. Below: the façade of the famous Cathedral. Following pages: aerial view of the Piazza dei Miracoli with the Leaning Tower, the Cathedral, the Baptistery and the *Campo Santo*.

At the northern edge of Pisa, the Piazza del Duomo – also known as the Piazza dei Miracoli – is the very archetype of Pisan-Romanesque art, and one of the most remarkable architectural groups one could ever hope to see !

The Baptistery, Duomo and Leaning Tower stand in isolation in the midst of lawns beyond the Porta Santa Maria – also known as the Porta Nuova.

The alternating colors of the marble, the rich decorative interplay of arcades and slender columns make a very striking picture, due both to the sheer artistic merit of the buildings and their location, just outside the town, as it were standing apart from time. Although they were built from the 11th to the 14th centuries, their originality and unity of style is clearly evident.

The visitor should spend a few hours studying and relishing the beauty of these three remarkable structures.

The Baptistery is a circular building which was started in 1153 in the Romanesque style. While work was proceeding on the upper part, the influence of the Gothic style was predominant ; the cupola was adorned with statues of the apostle and geometric patterns. The baptismal font and the pulpit, supported on seven marble columns decorated with symbols of the Virtues, date from the 7th century ; the pulpit is the work of Nicolo Pisano, the master of the Pisan school.

The Duomo, in the shape of a Latin cross, was consecrated in 1118, though its façade was not completed until the 13th. The coffered ceilings and a number of the murals were done after a fire in the 16th century. Here again, the wealth of decorative detail, the alternating colors of the marble, the fine quality of the sculptures and the bronze low reliefs on the doors, depicting scenes from the life of Christ and the Virgin, form a superbly harmonious whole.

In the interior, the pulpit by Giovanni Pisano (1302), which though damaged in the fire was rebuilt in 1926, is supported on columns of porphyry and sculpted pillars. The works of art in the choir include a bronze crucifix by Jean de Bologne and some paintings by Andrea del Sarto, in particular a deeply moving *Saint Agnes.*

The San Ranieri door faces the famous Leaning Tower, which is in the same Pisan-Romanesque style. It consists of six rows of slender columns which wind their way around the structure.Its elegant contours and the fact that it is leaning make it a unique piece of architecture. Various causes have been suggested for the tower's inclination, which Galileo put to good use when conducting his experiments on gravity. It seems likely, however, that it was deliberately built at an angle, which was calculated with such care that neither earthquakes not the bombardments of the Campo Santo proved able to shake the solidity of the Leaning Tower of Pisa.

On the north side of the square there is a burial ground dating from 1280, whose galleries are adorned with paintings by Benozzo Gozzoli, Taddeo Gaddi and a huge 14th-century fresco, *The Triumph of Death,* which is attributed to the Florentine school.

Pisa. Left: different details of the interior of the Cathedral and the Baptistery. Right: the Leaning Tower, famous throughout the world, and a view of the Piazza dei Miracoli, with the Baptistery in the foreground. Following pages: the towers of San Gimignano.

SAN GIMIGNANO AND ITS PRINCELY TOWERS

To the south of Florence and the Arno Valley, the Chianti hills are a prelude to the beauties of the artistic cities of the hinterland. This is a region of vine-clad hills whose name is among the most famous in Italy. Chianti, which is sold in paunchy straw-covered bottles, is much prized in its country of origin and abroad.

A brief trip to Greve and Castellina in Chianti, a leading wine-making center, will enable the visitor to taste the local growths, At Poggibonsi the road forks towards Siena and San Gimignano, where the traveler feels as if he has landed in the Middle Ages!

The best way to see San Gimignano, with its proud, princely towers high on the hill, is from the surrounding countryside. Fourteen towers now remain, though in the 14th century there were seventy-two. The building of these ostentatious structures was prompted by the ambitions of the leading families of the area, who thus enabled architectural science to strive to meet their challenge by producing ever bolder designs. Here again, however, discord between Guelphs and Ghibellines had disastrous consequences, causing the independent commune to come under Florentine rule.

A number of gates, formerly part of the fortifications, lead into the town. The Porta San Giovanni opens onto the Via of the same name, on which there are several 13th-century towers, the Palazzo Pratellesi, and the Becci archway and palace. We then emerge on the Piazza della Cisterna, in the heart of the town, where the old well is surrounded by the Salvestrini. Tortoli and other towers and palaces.

The nearby Piazza del Duomo makes an even more striking sight, with the Palazzo del Podesta (1239), the Chigi and Rognosa towers, the Salvacci Tower with its splendid loggia, the cathedral and the Palazzo di Popolo, whose 160-ft tower—the tallest in San Gimignano—has a terrace from which there is a magnificent view of the town and the surrounding countryside. The museum on the third floor contains works by Benozzo Gozzoli, Filippino Lippi, Filippino Pinturicchio and Guido da Siena.

The collegiate church—or Duomo—which is of Romanesque origin, was restored in the 19th

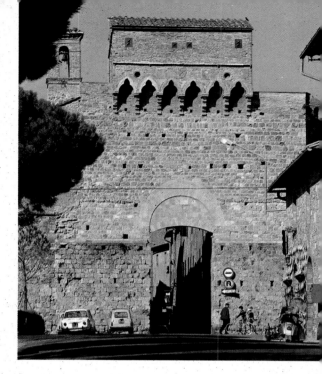

century. It has some frescoes by Gozzoli, and a number of local painters. The Santa Fina chapel (1468) is dedicated to the young saint who, at the age of ten, did penance by lying prostrate on a table, and died there five years later.

The church of St Augustine, in which the saint's life is depicted in frescoes by Gozzoli, the museum of sacred art and the Etruscan museum are also worth a visit. But the main appeal of San Gimignano lies in the charm of its old streets, its houses and its palaces, which combine nobility with grandeur. Here one truly streps back several centuries, beneath the bright blue sky, as the swallows swoop past overhead...

San Gimignano. Left: two views of the central square, called the Piazza della Cisterna. Opposite: the courtyard of the People's Palace and one of the doors of the ramparts. Photo below: when the innocence of the sheep is added to the purity of the Tuscan hillside...

SIENA – HISTORY, ART AND SAINTS

At the time of the Ghibellines, Siena was the rival of Florence. And it might still be, despite the fact that, in 1555, history attached it to the grand duchy of Tuscany, after a memorable siege! It certainly deserves to be thought of as a rival, by virtue of the wealth of its patrimony, the beauty of its monuments, and the charm of its old streets, where so many houses are in fact palaces!

"Burnt Siena", the color on the painter's palette, is named after the hills on which Siena is built, and those which surround it. As can be seen from the contents of its churches and museums, it has also given its name to a school of painting in which gentleness of feeling is combined with lightness of touch. Its representatives include Simone Martini, Pietro Lorenzetti, Stefano di Giovanni ("Sasetta"), and Il Sodoma, from Lombardy, who was a pupil of Leonardo da Vinci.

What Malaparte says about Tuscany in general is particularly true of Siena and its spiritual climate: "In Tuscany even the simplest, humblest, most ordinary things have a certain virtue which makes them miraculous."

Such a virtue was that of St Catherine, the mystic spouse of Christ, who had ecstasies and was stigmatized at Pisa in 1375, and who died, like her Master, at the age of thirty-three. In that same year, 1380, the future tough-minded reformer, St Bernardino, was born at Siena.

Writing of this delicate art and these vibrant souls, Malaparte enthused over the Sienese kindness of this "simple domestic civilization, half-bourgeois, half-peasant, a civilization of craftsmen, farmers, plowmen, market gardeners, millers, inn-keepers, wagoners, friars and nuns".

Legend had it that Siena was built by Senus, the son of Remus. And it is certainly true that the city's heraldic device does include the she-wolf and the twins, Romulus and Remus, the founders of Rome.

And independent republic in the 12th century, it clashed with Florence, having sided with the Ghibellines and triumphed in 1260. Ten years later, Charles of Anjou took the city and forced it into an alliance with the Guelph party. Then followed a succession of struggles and sieges, just as the beauty which we now admire in Siena was being created.

From the ramparts which still surround it there is a good view of the nearby red clay hills, truly the hue of "burnt Siena". The scallop-shaped Piazza del Campo, in the heart of the city, is paved with bricks with a pattern of light-colored stripes. This is the setting, on July 2 and August 16, for the famous Palio delle Contrade, with its procession of Sienese wearing 15th-century costumes, carrying banners and emblems. This is followed by the special Palio horse race, which is quite dangerous as it is run on the slippery paving stones. The winner is given the *Palio,* a banner bearing an image of the Virgin.

Siena. Top: the reddish clay of the region (from which the color "Burnt Siena" takes its name). Below: the beautiful ornamentation on the portico of the Chigi-Saracini Palace. Right: detail of a very ancient wooden door of the Public Palace; the facade and tower, 280 feet high, of the palace. Below: the famous Renaissance frescoes of the Public Palace. The palace leads out on to the remarkable Piazza del Campo.

Siena. The whole town takes part in the festival of the "Palio", the origin of which dates back to the Middle Ages, with its brightly-colored banners, its procession of 15th-century costumes and its lively horse races.

Next pages: Siena. The piazza del Campo, heart of the city.

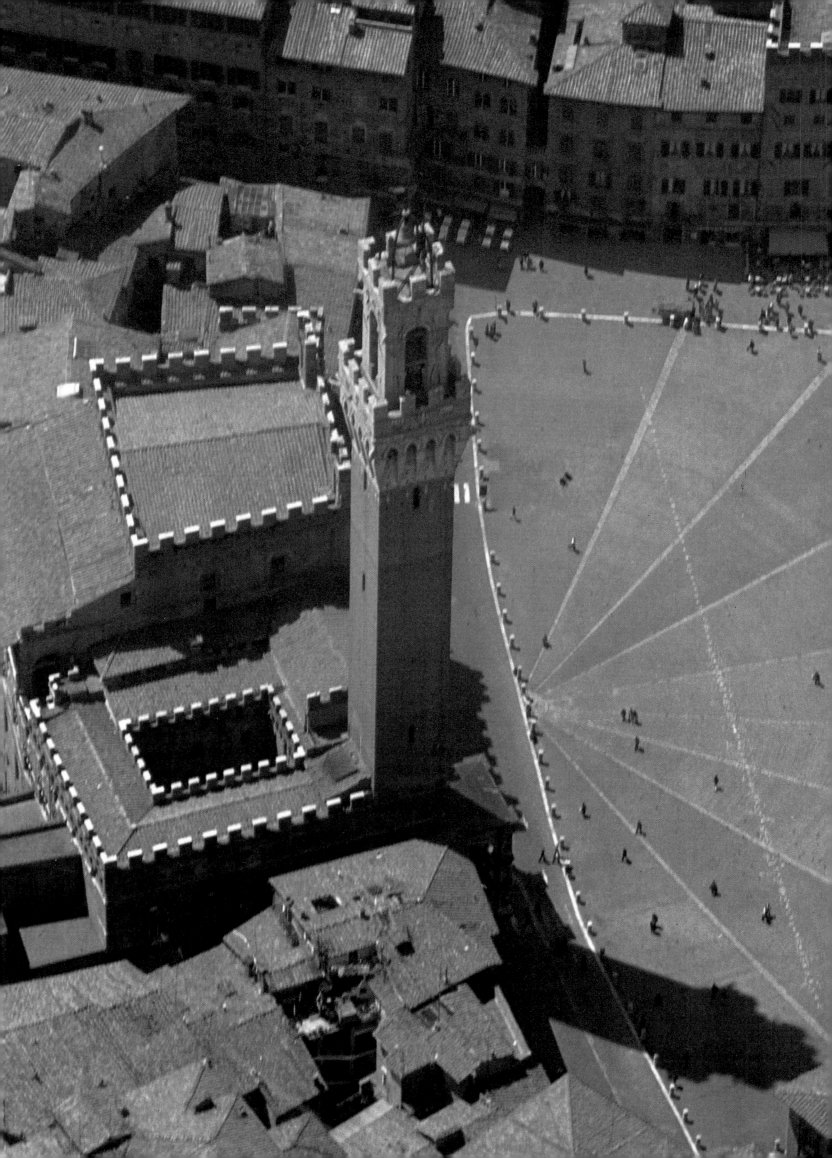

SIENA—FROM THE PIAZZA DEL CAMPO TO THE PIAZZA DEL DUOMO

Eleven streets lead into the Piazza del Campo, which is surrounded by a harmonious jumble of old houses with red tiled roofts and crenellated palaces. The early 15th-century Fonte Gaia (Fountain of Joy) is adorned with copies of the low reliefs of Jacopo della Quercia, the originals of which are in the palaces.

At the lower end of the square stands the Palazzo Pubblico, with its imposing brick façade and trilobate windows. The adjacent Torre del Mangia 286 ft.) was built between 1338 and 1348. The palace itself is in the Gothic style, and was built between 1288 and 1309, a number of additions being made in the middle of the 14th century. The chapel at the foot of the tower, which contains some statues of saints and frescoes by Il Sodoma, is of the same period.

The Palazzo Pubblico is now a magnificent museum, in which art is exhibited in the rooms in which the government of the nine consuls once sat. Interestingly enough, a series of frescoes by Ambrogio Lorenzetti depicting the effects of good and bad government is located in the Hall of Peace. In the Globe Room there is *Virgin with Baldacchino* by Simone Martini. Other exhibits include tapestries, sculptures and sacred *objets d'art*.

A few yards away, on the other side of the square, a stairway behind the fountain leads to the Loggia delle Mercenzia, the former mercantile court. It was built between 1417 and 1428 in a Gothic style with clear Renaissance overtones. The pillars are adorned with statues, and the vaulted ceiling with frescoes.

The other pole of attraction in Siena is the Piazza del Duomo, with the cathedral, the episcopal palace, the hospital of Santa Maria della Scala, partly of the 13th century, and the 16th-century Palazzo della Prefettura.

The Duomo, which was started in the 12th century in the Romanesque style, from plans drawn up by G. Pisano, was completed in the 14th century, under the influence of Gothic architecture. The alternating bands of white, black and red marble give the façade, and particularly the elegant campanile, whose openings become gradually wider from the bottom, a distinctively original appearance.

The interior of the Duomo is equally remarkable, first and foremost by virtue of its mosaics (15th and 16th centuries) depicting biblical scenes and allegories, now partly covered by a floor.

The breadth of the three naves, the alternating colors of the marble, the terra cotta images of the popes which adorn the cornice, and the hexagonal cupola with its galleries of slender columns all make up a striking picture, which is further enhanced by the statues of Donatello and the frescoes of Pinturicchio, as well as the pulpit by Nicolo Pisano, made between 1265 and 1268.

One's visit is completed by a walk around the Baptistery of San Giovanni (15th century), with baptismal fonts decorated with gilded copper low reliefs by Ghiberti, Donatello and Jacopo della Quercia. It is also worth while to visit the cathedral museum, located in another unfinished building, to which the present cathedral was to serve as a transept. It contains works by G. Piasno, Duccio and Simone Martini.

Siena. These two pages: the Duomo seen from different angles, so characteristic with its polychrome marble façade, the pictures in mosaic which cover the floor and its vaults entirely covered with ornamentation.

SIENA—CHURCHES AND PALACES; THE SIENESE SCHOOL

In Siena, as in Florence, the great religious orders—Franciscans and Dominicans—had their own churches, each of which reflects that order's spirit.

San Francesco is a composite building, construction having been spread out over a century and a half, from 1326 to 1475, but it was remodeled in the Baroque style in 1626 and restored at the end of the 19th century. The campanile dates from 1875 and the façade from 1913. The interior is decorated with frescoes by Lorenzetti and his studio.

The nearby monastery has a Renaissance cloister. The oratory of St Bernardino stands a short distance away on the site where the saint's eloquence used to stir the crowds.

At the other end of town is the enormous fortress-like brick church of San Domenico, which was built between 1226 and 1465, with a single nave, a campanile and a 14th-century triple-nave crypt. The "delle Vote" chapel, situated near the entrance, was where St Catherine took the Dominican habit in 1363 and experienced her ecstasies. A portrait of the saint by Andrea Vanni—said to be the sole authentic picture of St Catherine—hangs over the altar. The saint's chapel halfway along the nave has a Renaissance tabernacle containing her head. On the walls, frescoes by Il Somoda depict scenes from her life.

The house in which the saint was born is located in the street which bears her name, and has been enlarged by the addition of several oratories. The cell where she lived is on the lower floor.

The other religious buildings of Siena include the 12th-century church of St Augustine, the interior of which was renovated in the 18th century in the Baroque style. The Chapel of the Holy Sacrament contains frescoes by Ambrogio Lorenzetti, Matteo di Giovanni and Il Sodoma.

Santa Maria dei Servi, another 13th-century church, is well endowed with frescoes and sculptures, including a *Virgin of the People* by Lippo Memmi.

Besides churches, Siena is blessed with an abundance of palaces, particularly on the Via di Citta and the Via Bienchi di Sopra. The Palazzo Piccolomini dell Papesse is a Renaissance structure with an embossed stone façade and windows with

Romanesque arches. The Palazzo Chigi-Saracini has a particularly remarkable collection of paintings. The Salimbeni, Spennochi and Tantucci palaces, all in the same area, represent three different styles: Gothic, Baroque and Renaissance.

Lastly, the Palazzo Buonsignori (14th-century Gothic) houses the art gallery in which it is possible to follow the evolution of the Sienese school of painting, founded by Duccio. This heir to the Byzantine tradition brought the school to life by associating with it a more everyday observation of life. Pietro and Ambrogio Lorenzetti, Sassetta and his pupil Sano di Pietro, Domenico Beccafumi and Matteo di Giovanni are well represented. Only Simone Martini, of the masters of the Siena school, is missing from this prestigious gathering.

Siena. Left: the house where St. Catherine was born, a facade of the Palazzo Tolomei, a view of the "Fontebranda", erected in the 11th century, and two views over the roofs of the old town, beside the Cathedral. Above: loggia of the "Palazzo del Mangia". Opposite: the country around Siena.

VOLTERRA, THE CITY OF THE ETRUSCANS

The Etruscan civilization which developed in the heart of what is now Tuscany, around the 8th century B.C. is among those which scholars still find extremely puzzling. Were the Etruscans indigenous, or were they migrants from Lydia in Asia Minor? The question remains unanswered: though we do know that Etruria was a federation of communes among which Volterra seems to have been prominent, judging by the ruins of the Arco Etrusco, a gate made of huge stone blocks in the original fortified wall. Sculpted heads from the 3rd or 4th century B.C. can be seen on the gate.

Samples of this Etruscan art have been assembled in the Etruscan Museum, in particular more than 600 cinerary urns, ceramics and everyday objects from the last 400 years before the Christian era. The originality of this art lies in its blend of realism and stylized form, and above all in a sense of movement which is rarely found in the primitive arts.

The Etruscan Velathri, one of the twelve cities of the federation, became Volaterrae with the Roman conquest, and by the 12th century had the status of a commune.

Volterra's rich past survives mainly in its medieval character; its position on the top of a hill more than 1,500 ft. high gives it a scenic quality together with great majesty. Once inside the gates which still mark the position of the medieval fortifications, one can wander through its streets, past houses of warm-hued stone, some of them flanked by towers,

with occasional views of the fortress of Rocca Vecchia and Rocca Nuova.

The Piazza dei Priori, in the center of town, is surrounded by a cluster of former palaces, including that of the Priors (13th-century), which contains a fresco by Orcagna and a small museum of Tuscan painters, and also the Palazzo Pretorio with its twin windows and the adjacent Torre del Porcellino.

On the Piazza San Giovanni stands the Romanesque Duomo, which was started in 1120, and then enlarged and remodeled in the 13th and 15th centuries. The interior has three naves, with a handsome 13th-century pulpit, frescoes by Benozzo Gozzoli and alabaster stained-glass windows.

Alabaster is a specialty of Volterra. Today there are still many craftsmen who can be seen carving this beautiful translucent stone.

Via Sarti is lined with Renaissance palaces; the Piazza San Michele is graced by the splendid façade of its church and a house built like a tower. Lastly, running past the Fortezza and the archeological park is the Viale dei Ponti, which is a favorite walk of the Volterrans, with a view of the surrounding hills.

Volterra. Diana's Gateway, set in the Etruscan fortifications, and the Etruscan gateway to the town. Above: a farm in the surrounding countryside. Right: the old town overlooking a landscape of hills, the Roman theatre and the medieval fortress. Far right: terra-cotta coats-of-arms on the facade of a palace in Certaldo.

FROM CORTONA
TO MONTEPULCIANO AND CHIUSI

In the southeast of Tuscany, near the shores of lake Trasimeno, in Umbria, there are a number of other small towns which have preserved the memory of their past. They are often built on the sides or tops of hills, in a superb elevated position, overlooking broad plains and the glistening waters of the lake.

Cortona, for example, is situated at between 1,500 and 1,900 ft., the paving stones of its streets seemingly clinging to the steep slopes. The churches of San Domenico (15th-century), on the Piazza Garibaldi, contains a fresco attributed to Fra Angelico and some paintings, including a *Virgin surrounded by Saints,* by Luca Signorelli. This artist was born in Cortona in 1450, and died after a fall from scaffolding while painting a fresco on the walls of a neighboring villa.

The Via Nazionale leads into the center of town towards the Piazza della Repubblica, on which the Palazzo Communale is situated. This 16th-century structure, built over a 13th-century lower section, has a wide staircase leading up to it. There are a number of small squares, surrounded by fine monuments. Th Palazzo Casali (13th-century) contains an art gallery with works by Ghirlandaio, Pinturicchio and Signorelli, as well as Etruscan objects such as vases, jewlery and coins. the Duomo, situated nearby on a terrace overlooking the plain, was built in the 15th and 16th centuries, over the remains of an earlier church. The Diocesan Museum is located across the street in the church of the Gesu (15th and 16th-centuries). It contains an *Annunciation* by Fra Angelico, paintings of the Sienese school—Lorenzetti, Duccio, Sassatta—and several works by Signorelli.

The church of San Francesco was built on the initiative of Brother Elias, the companion of St Francis of Assisi, who was also the organizer of the Franciscan Order. His remains lie in the choir of the church, which was remodeled in the 17th century, and also contains some interesting paintings from the period.

St Margaret of Cortona is buried in the church rebuilt in the 19th century on an esplanade overlooking the town. It can be reached by a road which runs alongs the former ramparts, with fine views of the valley as far as Lake Trasimeno.

On the other side of the *autostrada* from Florence to Rome there are a number of small towns built on ancient stone. Asciano, in the Ombrone Valley, has a museum of sacred art and an Etruscan museum; Buon Convento is surrounded by ramparts with medieval gates; Montalcino lies in the shadow of a 13th-century *rocca* (feudal castle); and the abbey of Monte Oliveto Maggiore, superbly situated on the side of a cypress-clad hill, is well worth a visit. It comprises several buildings in the middle of a park, as well as a church and a cloister adorned with frescoes by Il Sodoma and Signorelli.

Further south is Montepulciano, richly endowed with Renaissance palaces, particularly on the Piazza Grande, where the Duomo is located; the resort town of Chianciano Terme and Sarteano, whose warm waters were already known to the Etruscans; and Chiusi, one of the towns of the Etruscan federation, which has a museum, and a number of Etruscan tombs in the surrounding countryside.

Left: the Municipal Palace of Cortona and the copper market in the town. Right: a delightful chapel (Santa Maria Nuovo) outside the town. The abbey of Sant-Antimo at Montalcino, surrounded by fields of red earth, and a view of the Tarugi Palace, on the main square of Montepulciano. Following pages: beautiful, noble and fertile: the Tuscan countryside...

THE APUAN ALPS
AND THE TUSCAN APENNINES

Carrara, a few miles from the coast road along the Tyrrhenian Sea, marks the boundary between the two Tuscan landscapes: the Riviera and its beaches, running from north to south, and the mountains forming a semicircle in the north of the province, in two parallel ranges—the Apuan Alps, inland from the coast, and the Tuscan Apennines, which stretch as far as the outskirts of Florence.

Carrara has a marina at the water's edge, while the town itself lies at the foot of the mountain. Its most notable features are a Romanesque-Gothic cathedral, an interesting art gallery, and, above all,

the marble quarries, which can be seen from the coast, glistening in the sun like glaciers. For many centuries, the mountain has yielded a variety of qualities of marble, the best being reserved for sculptors. It was here that Michelangelo came in person to select the blocks which he was to turn into his masterpieces!

There are several thermal spas in the interior: San Carlo Terme and Equi Terme, and some excellent walks can be taken along paths towards the peaks, which are about 6,000 ft. above sea level.

Massa, Seravezza, and Pietrasanta are located at the foot of the Apuan Alps. The Serchio Valley separates the Apuans from the Apennines, reach an altitude of 6,870 ft. at the Monte Giovo Pass and

7,036 ft. at the peak of Monte Cimone, where a mountain shelter is open. Hiking and winter sport are also available at the Abetone Pass, which has a cable-car which runs to Monte Gernito (6,150 ft.).

To the east, the mountain slopes down toward the opening through which the highway and a number of roads from Bologna to Florence pass.

Borgo San Lorenzo is one of the centers of the Mugello, in the Sieve Valley, which is separated by another range from the upper Arno Valley, o Casentino, one of the most picturesque regions of the mountains of Tuscany.

Bibbiena, 1,380 ft. up the side of the valley, is a market agricultural market town with a 15th century palace and some churches with low relief and frescoes. Above all, however, it is the point of departure for the Monastery of La Verna, situate in grim solitude in the midst of a forest, at 3,990 ft where St Francis received the stigmata of th passion of Christ in September 1224. Monks an pilgrims are housed in very substantial building The monastery church contains a number of terr cottas by members of the Della Robbia family including an admirable *Annunciation* by Andre Della Robbia. The Chapel of the Stigmata and th grotto containing the saint's cell can also be seen.

The peak of La Penna towers above the mona tery, at an altitude of 4,170 ft., overlooking a va mountainous panorama.

Above and right: two landscapes in the Apua alps. Left: the ancestral oxen help in the work the forest near Camaldoli; the campanile Carrara, known world-wide for its marble. Oppo site: the beautiful old town of Pontasieva.

AREZZO AND THE UPPER ARNO VALLEY

Arezzo is a town of Etruscan origin which was at one time called Arretium. Fighting and destruction were its lot in ancient times, as well as during the conflict between the Guelphs and Ghibellines. It has been the birthplace of a variety of famous men throughout the ages: Maecenas, the great patron of arts and letters; the Benedictine Giudo Monaco, inventor of musical notation; Pietro Aretino, the fearless writer; the poet Petrarch; Vasari, the painter and art historian; and numerous painters, including Margaritone.

In the upper part of the town one can see the house in which Petrarch was born; it was rebuilt in 1948 and now houses an Academy named after the poet. And also the Vasari Mansion, superbly decorated by the artist, and containing a collection of works by Tuscan painters.

The principal buildings and monuments of note are located in this same area, around two picturesque squares: Piazz della Liberta, with the 13th-century Gothic Duomo, which was remodeled in the 15th century, and the Palazzo Communale (14th-century), with its tower.

Slightly lower down is the Piazza Grande, bordered by medieval houses, with the prominent campanile of Santa Maria della Pieve, a Romanesque church remodeled by Vasari in the 16th century, and with a Pisan-Romanesque façade having three levels of slender columns. Behind these two squares are the Prato Gardens, which provide fine views of the local countryside and the remains of a 16th-century fort.

The Corso Italia, between the Piazza Grande and the boulevards which form the southern boundaries of Arezzo, becomes increasingly lively towards late afternoon, thronged with young people whose exuberance is still much in evidence in the early hours of the morning!

Among the other churches, art lovers should particularly note the 13th-century Gothic San Domenico, which has a Cimabue crucifix at the high altar, and, above all, San Francesco (14th and 15th centuries), its choir decorated with frescoes by Piero della Francesca on the Legend of the Holy Cross. It also contains works by Signorelli and Margaritone.

A Roman amphitheater from the 1st century B.C. and the nearby archeological museum are also worth a visit.

Arezzo is situated in the center of a broad valley, but the trip from Florence through the upper Arno Valley is most picturesque, taking one through a landscape of orchard-covered hills, fields of vines and olive trees, with the bluish contours of the Apennines closing the horizon.

Among the art-rich cities of the region, San Sepolcro, twenty miles away—is the home of Piero della Francesca; a polyptich by this artist can be seen in the former Palazzo Pretorio. The annual Palio dei Balestrieri, which is celebrated by persons dressed in the costumes of figures from his paintings, takes place in tribute to the painter.

By now we are in the valley of the Tiber, on the boundaries of Umbria. The Bocca Trabaria Pass (3,410 ft.) is where three regions meet: Tuscany, Umbria and the Marches.

Left: it was in this house at Arezzo that Petrarch was born. Below: an unusual view of the Apennines near S. Giovanni in the Val d'Arno. This page: Arezzo, the Palazzo Pretorio and the Palazzo dei Priori, built in the 14th century. A farm in the neighbouring countryside.

The vineyards of Tuscany are famous and the vines add to the charm of the countryside (opposite). Left, bottom: the Castle of Brolio. Above: an ancient wine-press. Below: the grape-harvest.

THE TUSCAN RIVIERA AND LEGHORN

After the artistic cities and the Apennine range, the Tuscan seashore, or Riviera, is the province's third face. It may be the least characteristic, but it is certainly not the least attractive for visitors who come looking for sun-drenched beaches and, here and there, wild inlets.

A number of recent, well-equipped resorts are strung out from north to south, their huge beaches reaching up to the pine forests next to the mountain slopes, or elsewhere along the coast, stretching as far as the hills of the hinterland.

In the north, the Apuan Alps protect the coastal areas from the cold winds. Each town has its own "marina": Marina di Carrara, Marina di Massa, usually separated from the interior by pine forests, orchards or croplands. The proximity of the mountains makes these resorts especially attractive.

The Apuan Riviera continues southwards in the form of the Versilia Riviera, with three well-known resorts: Forte dei Marmi, Marina di Pietrasanta, Lido di Camaiore and, in particular, Viareggio, one of the finest beaches in Italy, enclosed by a magnificent pine forest, and with a splendid avenue of lime trees. The coast road runs between the sea and the pine grove, linking up the various resorts.

South of Viareggio, lakes have formed since the draining of coastal marshlands: they include Lake Massaciuccoli, where surfboarding and waterskiing are practised, and Lake Puccini, near which one can visit the museum dedicated to the famous composer, who lived for many years in this house and wrote several of his operas there.

Marina di Pisa, further south again, lies at the mouth of the Arno. This is the beach of the inhabitants of Pisa, as is Tirrenia, which is situated in the pine grove, with playing fields and golf courses. Tirrenia was much used for the production of Italian films in the 50s.

The great port of the Tuscan Riviera is Leghorn, home town of Amadeo Modigliani. a naval academy was founded there in 1881. The old part of this lively town is situated behind the port. The Duomo dates from 1595 and has a marble portico. The Viale Italia runs along the water's edge as far as the seaside resorts of Ardenza and Antignano.

Thereafter the coast stretches away almost in a straight line as far as Piombino, with coastal resorts such as Castiglioncello, which has an Etruscan museum, Cecina Mare and San Vicenzo, from which it is possible to see the island of Elba.

Above: a view of the Fortezza Vecchia at Leghorn. Left: a palace in the famous resort of Viareggio, the house of Puccini at Torre del Lago, and a view of the Tuscan Riviera at Punta Ala. Right: the beach of Marina di Carrara and Lake Massaciuccoli.

The boat comes in at Portoferraio, the island['s] capital, whose houses cling to the rocky slopes. Th[e] Baroque church of San Cristino contains som[e] mementoes of the emperor, whose house is open t[o] visitors in summertime.

From Portoferraio a number of roads lead to th[e] other resorts on the island, passing through a prett[y] landscape of orchards and undergrowth. After th[e] brightly colored houses of Portoliveri, we come t[o] Porto Azzuro, nestling between two rocky hea[d]dlands. Paths lead up to the San Giacomo For[t] built in 1603 by Philip II of Spain.

The road continues northwards to Rio Marin[a] and Rio nell'Elba, at 490 ft. The local iron mine[s] were worked in ancient times.

Another interesting route takes us around th[e] western part of the island, via San Marino, site [of] the Villa Napoleone, the emperor's summer resi[-]dence, in which his private apartments are open t[o] the public.

Marciana Marina is a seaside resort five mile[s] from Marciana, a picturesque village at the foot o[f] Mt. Capanna. The Madonna del Monte Chape[l] and the small adjacent house are a reminder of th[e] meeting between Napoleon and Countess Wa[-]lewska in September 1814. Lastly, in the south o[f] the island, Marina del Campo has a beach and [a] harbor which are well sheltered from the nort[h] winds.

FROM PIOMBINO TO THE ISLAND OF ELBA

Piombino, at the tip of a peninsula which closes off the Gulf of Follonica, is a small industrial town which, apart from its Palazzo Communale, with a 16th-century tower, is interesting only as the port from which boats leave for Elba.

In 1805, still displaying his customary generosity with the spoils of conquest, Napoleon had given his sister Elisa the principality of Piombino. Nine years later, he found himself appointed—by his victorious enemies—sovereig of the island of Elba. He reigned there for less than a year, being too ambitious to content himself with such a modest empire! On February 20, 1815, he slipped away from the island, in order to try one last grand venture.

Elba is now well within the range of even the lowliest pocket-book, judging by the large numbers of people who pile every week-end into the big boats or the *aliscafi* (hydrofoils) which make the crossing. As one approaches the island a few islands appear, then the coastline of Elba itself, and its hills and mountains, clad in undergrowth. The jagged

Top left: the little harbor of Piombino. Below: the *villa dei Mulini,* **where Napoleon lived while on the island of Elba. Right: Portoferraio, capital of the island, and the harbor of Porto Azzurro, on the east coast.**

The island of Elba. Roman remains at Porto Azzurro. Below: the bay of Cavoli. Right: a mountain landscape. Below: a villa once occupied by Napoleon at S. Martino, and the beach at Fetovia.

GROSSETO AND THE MAREMMA RIVIERA

Maremma, to the south of Piombino, also has a riviera of sandy beaches shielded by the pine groves which were planted after this once swampy area had been drained. There are a few rocky outcroppings here and there: Punta Ala and the Talamone Promontory, at the foot of the Uccellina Mountains, in the south.

Follonica, a small and lively resort, has given its name to the gulf which enclosed it. Beyond Punta Ala, Castiglione della Pescaia, an old fishing village, is also a tourist center connected to Riva del Sole, a very popular recent resort.

In the Ombrone Valley, Grosseto, the chief town of the Maremma region, is an old city of Etruscan origin. Its 16th-century ramparts have been turned into a promenade, passing near the towering citadel, of the same period, to the east. There are number of medieval structures in the center of town: the Duomo (1250), with a marble façade which was restored in the 19th century; the church of St Francis, also of the 13th century, with some remnants of frescoes and a fine cloister; and, lastly,

a museum of sacred art and an archeological museum which contains Etruscan and Roman objects.

Grosseto, which is eight miles inland, also has its marina. Principina a Mare and Marina di Alberese, their hotels and villas built among the pines, are located on either side of the mouth of the Ombrone.

The Maremma Riviera extends as far as the peninsula of Monte Argentario (2,030 ft.), whose slopes, clad in undergrowth, and groves of olive, orange and lemon trees, rise on all sides near the sea. An isthmus—known locally as *tomboli*—separates Monte Argentario from the coast and from the lagoon on which Orbetello, with its remains of Etruscans walls, is located. Two roads lead to the villages on the peninsula: Porta San Stefano, in the

Left: a village (Montegiovi) in the province of Grosseto. Below: the fine pine-forest of Castiglione della Pescaia. Right: remains of a Roman villa at Giannutri and the peninsula of Punta Ala. Below: a view of the Canal of the Marina di Grosseto.

orth, clinging to the mountainside, and Porto
rcole, in the south, guarded by a number of old
panish forts.

The Maremma Riviera also comprises some
lands. The main one, some twelve miles from
Mt. Argentario, is the island of Giglio, from which
here is a boat service to Porto San Stefano. There
re a few fishing villages nestling in inlets along the
oast. Further out to sea, is the island of Giannutri;
nd, south of Elba, Pianosa and the island of
Monte Cristo, which Alexandre dumas revealed to
he world. In the words of a local guide, here there
re "rocks, shrubs and wild goats, with no roads, no
rt and no modern comforts". One thing the area
oes have, however, is the wild natural surroun-
ings of another age.

Left: three views of the "Maremma", an ancient
marshy region near the sea, with its canals and its
orses. Above: the coast at Orbetello. Right: Porto
rcolo. Last page: a vista on the Tuscan hills from
an Gimignano.